Lit STITCH

25 CROSS-STITCH PATTERNS *for* BOOK LOVERS

Book Riot

Abrams × New York

xx

CONTENTS

xxxxxxxxxxxxxxxxxxxxxxxxxxxxxxxxxxxxxxxxxxxxxxxxxxxxxxxxxxxxxxxxxxxx

Introduction

In the world of pastimes, there are hobbies, and then there are passions—interests so deep and extensive that they infuse our identities and inform the way we see the world. Books? Well, books are a passion.

When you're a reader, books aren't just something you enjoy every now and then, they're a constant. Books are your entertainment, your escape, and your education. You talk about books, you probably join more book clubs than you can keep up with, you try to read the book before you see the movie, and your friends are definitely used to hearing you say, "Oh, I just read a book about that!"

Being a book lover is, as the kids say, a whole thing. But it's not the only thing! Books make the world bigger, and readers are a curious and interested lot. Book people are also into music and art and artisanal coffee and the art of French cooking and rock climbing and yoga, and, yes, some book people are into cross-stitching. There's been a real revival of handicrafts across generations in recent years, and much like literature, some of the more traditional forms—like cross-stitch—have been revived and reshaped for pop culture.

That's where you come in.

Whether you're a casual stitcher, a gold medal expert, or picking up a needle and thread for the very first time (look at you, trying something new!), you'll find designs for your skill level and personality here. Some are silly, some are sweary, and some are even a little bit serious. We've got everything from flowers to skulls, delicate cursive to neon lights. There are stacks on stacks. Spines. Shelves. Classic quotes and modern Book Riot slogans. Dinosaurs AND wine, because you shouldn't have to choose.

Accessibility and inclusivity are core values at Book Riot, so cross-stitching is a perfect craft for our merry band of book lovers. Embroidery floss is relatively inexpensive, and aida fabric (the traditional fabric for cross-stitch) isn't too pricey, either. And technically, you don't even have to have aida fabric; you can use anything with a visible weave! The internet makes creating and sharing patterns and finding a crafting community super easy. You don't need any drawing or design skills to get started, but if you have those skills, you can alter these designs however you like. The best books meet us where we are, and so does cross-stitching!

Bonus: cross-stitch makes for excellent bookmarks.

Every design is accompanied with a detailed chart and suggested colors, but they're just that: suggestions. Follow the rules, or add your own embellishments. Change the colors. Stitch in a little flair. Your bookshelf is a reflection of your personality, and your bookish cross-stitches should be, too. What we're trying to say is: you do you.

Grab your favorite snack, put on your favorite playlist—or an audiobook, if multitasking is your jam—and get to stitching.

About This Book

We took some of our favorite, most badass literary designs and turned them into fun, easy-to-make cross-stitch patterns. And there's something for everyone here: a friendly **Bookasaurus** to hang on your wall, or a bookmark that plainly gets across your motto of **Read a Fucking Book**. Show your love for someone with **ISBN Thinking of You** or your more rebellious side with **Readers Resist**. They're all good choices, we think.

First up, we've included an introductory guide to the craft of cross-stitch: what you need to know, the materials you'll need, basic techniques to get you started, and how to wrap up a piece and display when all's said and done.

And then there are the patterns themselves, each with a photograph of the finished piece, as well as the color-coded chart so you can replicate the pattern with ease. You know you want one of these up on your wall—or at your desk or holding your spot in your latest read—so, really, the only thing left to do is start stitching!

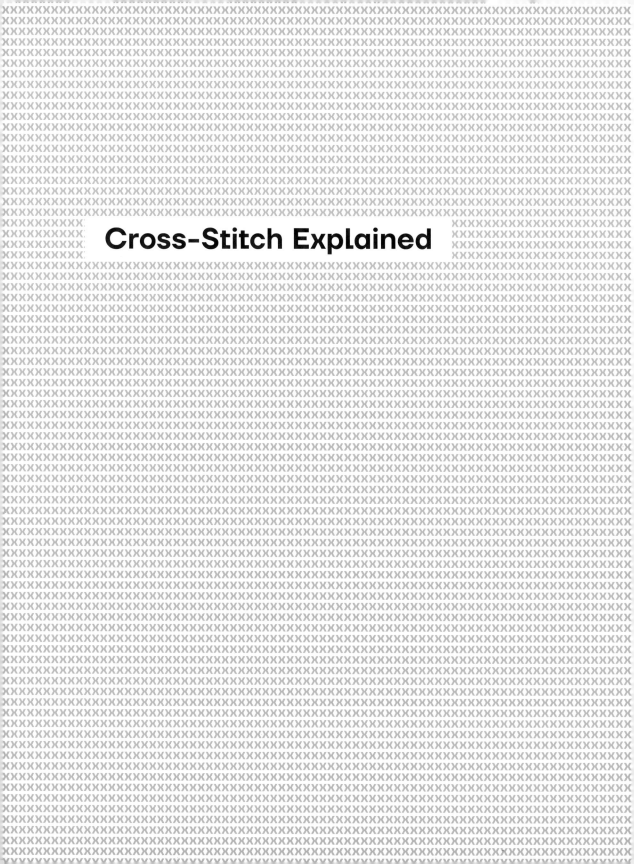

Cross-Stitch Explained

the materials

WHAT YOU HAVE TO HAVE

Fabric

Though you can cross-stitch on any fabric, the most commonly used for cross-stitching is aida fabric. Aida fabric is made for cross-stitch. It's sturdy and has a perfect square grid of holes for you to complete your stitches. You can find aida fabric in all major craft stores in a variety of colors.

All aida fabrics have a "count." This count refers to the number of squares per inch. The most common size you'll find in major craft stores is 14 count, meaning 14 squares per inch. All of the finished dimensions of the patterns in this book are given assuming you're using a 14-count fabric.

If you'd like your finished piece to be larger or smaller than what's mentioned here, you can stitch it on a different count fabric. Just remember that the higher the count, the smaller the finished piece.

You can calculate the size of your piece based on this formula:

Num of stitches tall/wide in the pattern
÷ count of the fabric
= number of inches of the finished piece

So, if a pattern is 150 stitches wide and completed on 18-count fabric, the end piece will be about 8⅓ inches (21 cm) wide.

Aida fabric is usually sold in rolls. You'll want to buy enough fabric to fit your piece's final framed size with about 1½ inches (3.75 cm) extra on every side. For example, if you want to frame your piece in an 8-inch (20 cm) hoop, you'll want a piece of fabric at least 11 inches × 11 inches (28 cm × 28 cm).

Needle

Cross-stitch is typically done with a tapestry needle. A tapestry needle is different from a standard sewing needle that you might find in a sewing kit in two important ways. First, the end is relatively blunt. Aida fabric already comes with grid holes in it, so the needle doesn't need to be sharp. As a bonus, you won't accidentally poke yourself! Secondly, a tapestry needle's eye is much larger than a sewing needle's. Embroidery thread is thicker than sewing thread, so a bigger eye is needed. Another bonus: Tapestry needles are easier to thread!

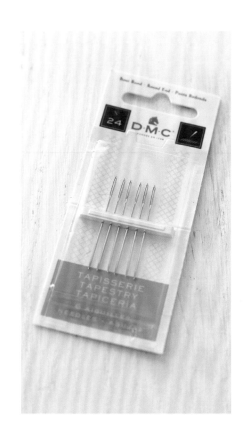

Tapestry needles come in different sizes that correspond to the diameter of the needle. Depending on what count fabric you have chosen, you'll want to choose a tapestry needle of a matching size. The larger the grid on the fabric, the larger the needle. One thing to avoid, though, is a needle that is too big. A bigger needle may stretch out the threads of the fabric and make it a little holey.

6-count aida fabric	Size 18
8-count aida fabric	Size 20
11-count aida fabric	Size 22
14-count aida fabric	Size 24
16-count aida fabric	Size 26
18-count aida fabric	Size 28

Embroidery Floss

All the patterns in this book use DMC brand embroidery floss and the DMC floss color codes. DMC is the most commonly found embroidery thread and can be found at any major craft store.

AND THEN THE ONES WE SUGGEST

Embroidery Hoop

Aida fabric is sturdy enough that you could manage to stitch while holding it with just your hands; however, using an embroidery hoop to keep the fabric super taut is easier and will keep your hand from cramping!

There are many kinds of embroidery hoops: round plastic hoops, round wooden hoops, and even square snap frames ideal for larger pieces of fabric. As you continue on your stitching journey, you might want to experiment and find what works best for you. However, if you plan on framing your finished piece in a hoop, a wooden one can do double duty and be used for both stitching and framing.

Other

Some materials that aren't absolutely necessary to get started but can certainly come in handy include:

× **A pair of small embroidery scissors.** These have a fine, sharp tip, which is great for snipping those tiny thread ends.

× **A needle threader.** For most stitchers, threading by hand is manageable due to the large eyes of tapestry needles. However, if you are having any trouble, grab a needle threader. They are quite cheap!

x **Water-soluble marker.** Especially for larger projects, some stitchers like to draw guidelines every ten rows/columns to make counting easier. Water soluble markers, which can be found in the sewing section of craft stores or at fabric stores, wash away easily once the stitching is done.

x **Materials for framing/finishing.** No matter if you choose to frame your work in a picture frame, an embroidery hoop, or if you make one of the bookmarks in this book, there are some additional materials you may want to have on hand to give your masterpiece a more finished, polished look. These can include cardstock, acid-free double-sided tape, felt, or self-adhesive mounting board. More on this in "Framing Your Piece" on page 35.

getting started with stitching

Cross-stitch is actually a pretty simple, straightforward craft. The gridded fabric used requires a lot less dexterity than freehand embroidery, and the built-in squares make for easy counting (and make it significantly easier to keep track of where you are). There are a few tips and tricks, though, that, when mastered, give you all the skills necessary to complete any cross-stitch pattern that you put your mind to, and may even help you devise a few of your own.

THE TWO BASIC RULES OF CROSS-STITCH

Though the cross-stitch community, especially in the fun and contemporary age of cross-stitch, is pretty easygoing, there are two hard-and-fast rules.

1. **All of your crosses should be crossed in the same order.** Each stitch is made of a "forward" diagonal and a "backward" diagonal. In your final piece, all the diagonals of one kind should lie under all of the opposite diagonals. It doesn't matter which kind goes on top, it just matters that the stitches are consistent. More on this on page 23.

2. **No knots.** In other kinds of sewing, you may tie a knot in your thread to keep it secured. However, in cross-stitch, we use fancy tucking to keep all the thread ends in place. More on this on page 28.

There is a third, more lax rule in cross-stitch, though we view it as a more of a guideline than something to get too hung up on.

3. **Keep the back tidy.** Many experienced cross-stitchers pride themselves on keeping the back of their work tidy. Some even say the back of your work should be as presentable as the front. And there is some practicality in putting thought and effort into keeping the back neat. Neatness can make stitching easier, especially in patterns with many colors interspersed with one another. But most importantly, do what works best for you. If you'd like the back to look as perfect as possible, go for it! If the thought of striving for perfection stresses you out, feel free to move on (you can always hide the back, so no one will be any the wiser).

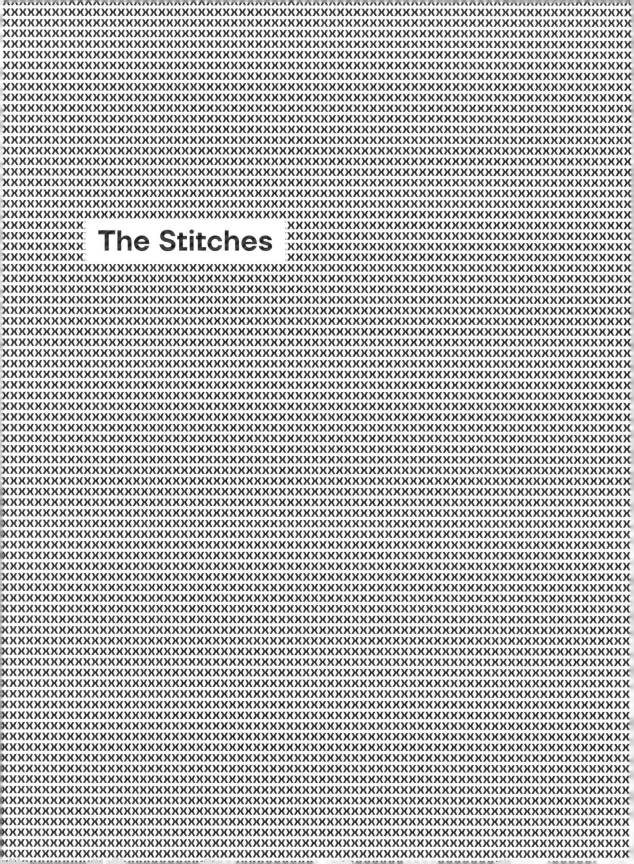

The Stitches

The patterns in this book are made up of two kinds of stitches: the basic cross-stitch and the backstitch.

the cross-stitch

One basic cross-stitch is comprised of two diagonals. You'll start with your needle and thread in the back of the fabric and pull it through to the front through one of the holes in the grid. Then, from the front of the fabric, push your needle back through the hole diagonally down and to the right.

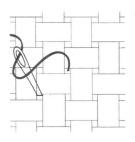

Then pull your thread from back to front on the upper right hole of the square. And finally, push your needle and thread from front to back in the lower left hole of the square.

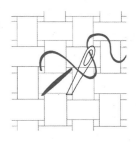

Again, it doesn't matter which diagonal you complete first so long as you are consistent throughout your piece.

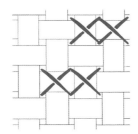

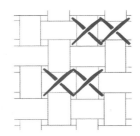

When a pattern has multiple stitches of a color in a row, you should do the whole row in just one of the diagonals first, and then complete the whole row of opposite diagonals.

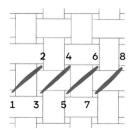 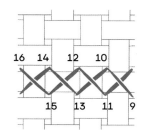

A note on keeping your work tidy: as you work across the row, starting each diagonal from the same corner every time (e.g., always from the bottom left of the square) will keep the back looking tidier, as shown here.

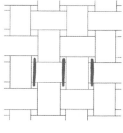

If you switch it up and sometimes start from the bottom left, sometimes from the top right, the back may look a bit haphazard, like it does here.

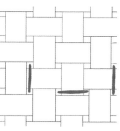

But hey, it's the front that counts, so if you want to keep it business in the front and party in the back, go for it!

When a pattern has a whole chunk of one color, you can take the same approach and do several rows' worth of one of the diagonals first (option 1) or you can do it row by row (option 2). Do what works for you!

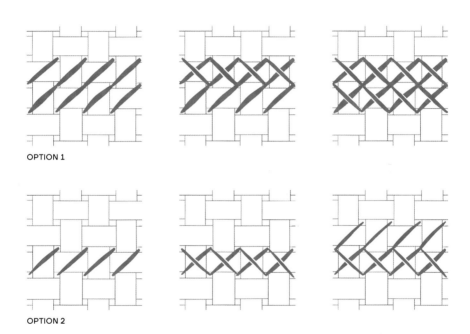

OPTION 1

OPTION 2

the backstitch

The backstitch is for making continuous lines and is used for some text and outlines. A single stitch of backstitch will either go along one side of a square in the grid or across the diagonal of a square in the fabric, whatever your pattern calls for.

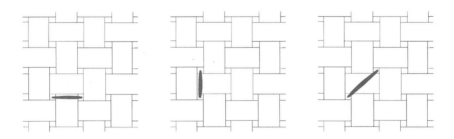

When you add another stitch of backstitch to your continuous line, you come up from the back of the fabric one square away from the existing line and stitch backward to connect the two. This is what puts the "back" in backstitch.

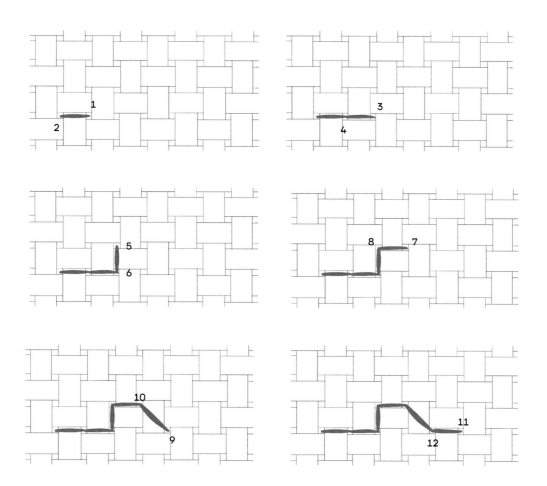

no knots: starting and stopping threads

One of the rules of cross-stitch is that you should never knot your thread. Instead, there are methods to secure your threads without knotting them by hiding the ends underneath the backs of stitches.

To start a thread off, thread your needle and pull it through your fabric from back to front, but do not pull it all the way through. Leave a 1-inch (2.5-cm) tail hanging in the back and hold it down securely with your finger. Then complete the first stitch, passing the needle from front to back. Then, when you begin your second stitch from back to front, ensure that the back of this second stitch loops over the tail, thereby closing over it and securing it:

Continue to secure the tail with the backs of the next few stitches. The back of your work will look like this:

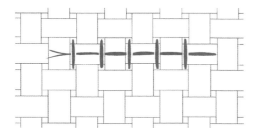

To secure your thread tail at the end of stitching, simply slide your needle and thread under the backs of your stitches and pull all the way through. We recommend snipping off excess thread as close as possible, leaving a short thread end to prevent any knots as you continue stitching. This is where a pair of small embroidery scissors can come in handy.

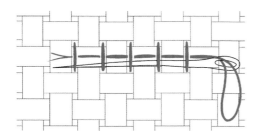

Making a Piece

prepping your materials

EMBROIDERY FLOSS

We recommend cutting your floss into working lengths of 12–18 inches (32–46 cm). Any longer and the thread will get easily twisted and tangled; any shorter and you'd be switching threads too often.

If you inspect your floss, you'll see that it is actually composed of six strands twisted together. We typically do not stitch with all six strands, so you'll have to separate a smaller group of strands to work with. If you like a more dimensional, full-square look for your stitches, use more strands. If you like a more sparse look that really emphasizes the X shape of your stitches, use fewer strands:

14-count aida fabric	2–3 strands
16-count aida fabric	2 strands
18-count aida fabric	1–2 strands

To separate threads, pinch the floss about half an inch from one end. Tap directly on the end of the floss with your other hand and you'll see the strands start to unravel. From there, you can divide the strands by pulling your finger through the length of the thread, somewhat similar to how you might part hair in order to braid it.

Because cross-stitch uses only one to two strands for most projects, you can get more yardage out of your skeins. Each skein is about 8.7 yards in total. So, if you're only using one strand for a project, you will actually be able to get more than 52 yards of embroidery floss per skein. Most of the projects in this book require only one skein per color per project, so a little can truly go a very long way. Keep in mind that the yardage per project here is also reflective of one strand. So for Read Harder (page 47), you will stitch with two strands together and need 18.8 yards of floss to complete the project, which means in total you will use 37.6 yards. Due to embroidery floss's very low cost, feel free to err on the side of buying more if you're worried about the amount needed—we've got enough projects to help you bust through any leftovers you may have!

FABRIC

Cut your fabric to be 1½ inches (4 cm) larger on each side than your finished piece. If you are using a colored fabric, wash and dry it before starting your project to prevent any color bleeding.

We recommend starting to stitch from the center of the pattern, aligning it with the center of the fabric. This way, you can ensure that your final stitched pattern is centered, leaving enough fabric to complete the entire piece and have a border for framing, etc. To find the center of the fabric, simply fold the fabric in half both ways. You can mark the center with a water-soluble marker, very light pencil mark, or even just by creasing it really well.

how to read a pattern

Each full square on a cross-stitch pattern represents one basic cross-stitch. Basic cross-stitches make up the majority of most cross-stitch patterns, and you should stitch all basic cross-stitches first.

Your pattern may also have some thick lines throughout; these represent backstitches. Any backstitch should be stitched after and over the basic cross stitches.

dealing with mistakes

Mistakes happen! But worry not, we can fix them.

When a mistake is not a mistake. Getting a stitch or two wrong from the pattern may not be worth going back and fixing. For example, in the toucans in the Borges quote pattern (see page 94), if you accidentally stitch one shade of turquoise where a slightly darker shade of turquoise was supposed to go, it probably won't be noticeable to anyone. If you miscount and make one of the books in the Jane Austen quote pattern (page 74) a stitch longer than the pattern says, you can probably just let that slide.

Accidental missing stitches. If the mistake you made was omitting stitches, you can always go back and add them later, easy peasy.

Accidental extra stitches. If you've accidentally added an extra stitch in a place that really sticks out, such as in stitching text, you will need to undo those stitches.

If the mistake happened with the thread you are still currently working with, you can unpick the errant stitches. It's tempting to want to "unstitch" those stitches by reversing your steps with the needle still threaded, but you can potentially create knots by doing so. Instead, remove your needle from the thread, then use the needle to undo the stitch by pulling on stitches from the front of the work.

If the mistake happened on a previous thread and unraveling it is too daunting of a task, you'll have to cut the thread. It's a bummer, but sometimes it has to be done. Snip the thread from the front of the work to ensure you don't accidentally snip any neighboring stitches. Unravel enough thread on both sides of the snip so that you can securely tuck those ends on the back of the work, then restitch the section.

framing your piece

After all that hard work stitching (congrats!), your piece deserves to be framed nicely and hung in a place of honor.

WASHING YOUR PIECE

As you stitch, your piece may get a bit dirty from your hands or your environment (we're fans of stitching in public and during commute-time). You'll want to wash your piece with mild soap (dish soap or baby soap works great) in cold to tepid water to prevent any bleeding of the colors. You can fill a tub or sink with soapy water and do some gentle swishing. If some areas of the fabric are particularly dirty, you can apply soap on your finger, or even a clean toothbrush, and scrub the offending area. Try to keep any heavier scrubbing or direct soap application just to the fabric and not to the stitches themselves. Lay on a clean towel to dry.

If the fabric has any wrinkles, you can iron it. Use your cotton setting and iron the piece facedown, with a towel underneath, so you don't squash any of your beautiful stitches.

FRAMING IN A HOOP

Framing your piece in a wooden hoop not only looks cute, but at $2 to $3 a pop, it can be a lot cheaper than a picture frame.

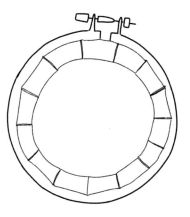

The absolute simplest way to frame is to hoop your piece, making sure it's centered. Then, from the back, simply trim all excess fabric. While easy, this is also a bit irreversible, so only choose this method if you are absolutely sure you'll never want to reframe it in a different way.

For a more forgiving option, you can keep the excess fabric untrimmed and instead fold it down and secure it with acid-free double-sided tape applied to the inner rim of the hoop.

Our favorite and recommended way to frame in a hoop involves a couple more steps but yields a really nice finished product, perfect for gift-giving.

1. Using the inner rim of the hoop, trace and cut a piece of cardstock in the same color as your fabric.

2. Repeat step 1 with a piece of felt in the same color as your fabric.

3. Hoop your piece, ensuring it is centered.

1. Place the cardstock against the back of your work. The cardstock provides a nice opaque background.

2. Line the inner rim of the hoop with double-sided tape.

3. Fold in the excess fabric, pressing it into the tape to secure it.

4. Attach the felt circle with a bit more double-sided tape. The felt hides all the raw edges of the fabric.

FRAMING IN A FRAME

Most people frame their cross-stitch pieces without the glass. We actually like to use the glass itself as the backing for the piece. Not only does it mean you don't have to find a piece of scrap cardboard to use instead, you also don't have to find a place to keep or discard the random piece of glass. To frame, simply center your piece on the glass and secure tightly with double-sided tape. For an extra solid/opaque look, you can cut a piece of matching cardstock to the size of the glass and secure that with double-sided tape to the glass before attaching the fabric.

BOOKMARK INSTRUCTIONS

1. After washing, drying, and ironing the piece, fold the extra width of the fabric back so that the edges overhang a tiny bit. Use the weave of the fabric as a guide to make the folds nice and straight. You can crease the folds with an iron, but simply using your fingers also works fine.

2. Trim the overhang so that the edges meet perfectly in the middle.

3. Fray the top and bottom edges by pulling a vertical thread out of the fabric. We like to fray ten rows' worth of fabric, leaving ten rows of un-frayed fabric on either side of the finished design, but feel free to experiment with the length as you see fit.

4. Trim your fabric adhesive or fusible interfacing to fit the un-frayed portion of the bookmark and attach it according to the package's instructions.

5. When folding the back flaps over the adhesive, be sure to align the edges neatly in the middle.

6. Cover the seam with a piece of matching ribbon and some fabric glue if desired.

AND NOW,

page 42

page 47

page 50

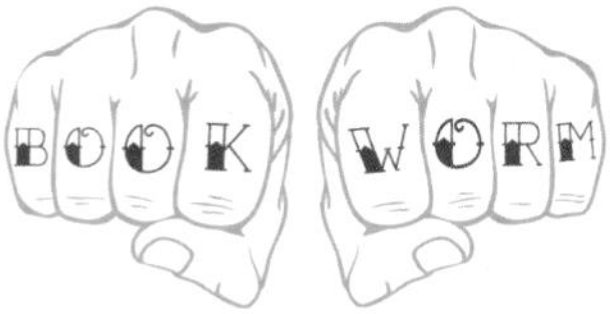

page 54

page 59

page 62

page 67

page 70

page 74

page 79

page 82

page 86

page 91

the Projects

page 94

page 98

page 103

page 107

page 110

page 114

page 119

page 122

page 127

page 130

page 135

page 138

Whether the question is how to start a normal day or which destination to visit first on vacation, the answer is the same: **Everything else sounds nice, but first, books.** Your priorities are set in stone, so you might as well set them in stitches, too.

BUT
FIRST,
BOOKS

10:53

Broil

Timer
Set/On

Select
Clean

Oven
Preheat
Door Locked

xxxxxxx   DMC 791   Very Dark Cornflower Blue   2 strands   34.48 yards

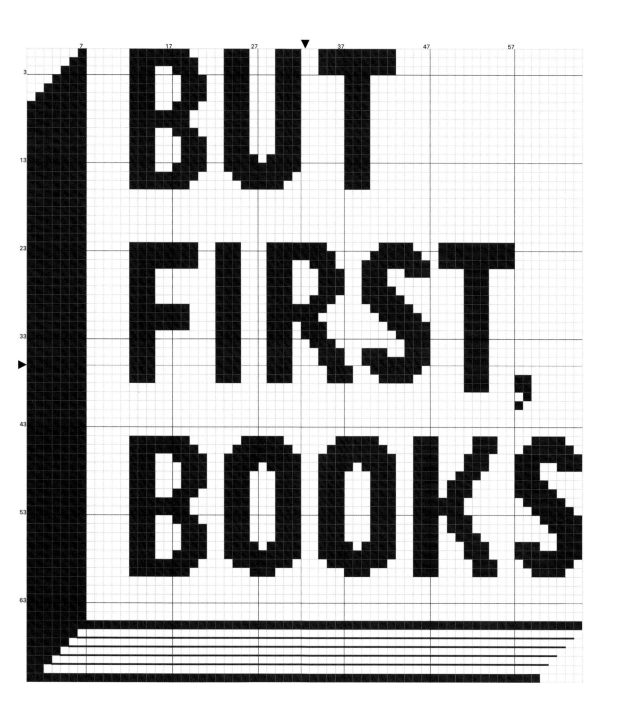

This is the Book Riot motto that launched a movement!

We created the Read Harder Challenge in 2015 to help readers get out of their comfort zones and get more out of their reading lives: more diversity, more genres, more adventure, more education, more of all the things that make books so important and powerful. You know all the times you find yourself thinking,

I wish I could read more?

Read Harder is about that desire. If you're always looking for more books to read, more time to read, more ways to make books part of your everyday, Read Harder is your jam. And if you want to join the challenge, visit us at bookriot.com/readharder.

XXXXXXX   **DMC 728**   Golden Yellow   **2 strands**   **18.8 yards**

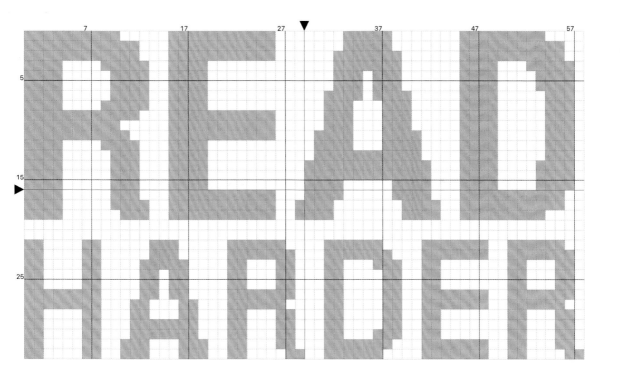

They say that anticipation of pleasure is even better than experiencing the thing you've been anticipating. We don't know if that's always the case, but we're pretty sure there are few things in life more enjoyable than the moment right before you start reading a new book. You open the cover, take in that new-book smell, and prepare to dive into a new world.

When you're a reader, the action is right there, between the covers.
Get some.

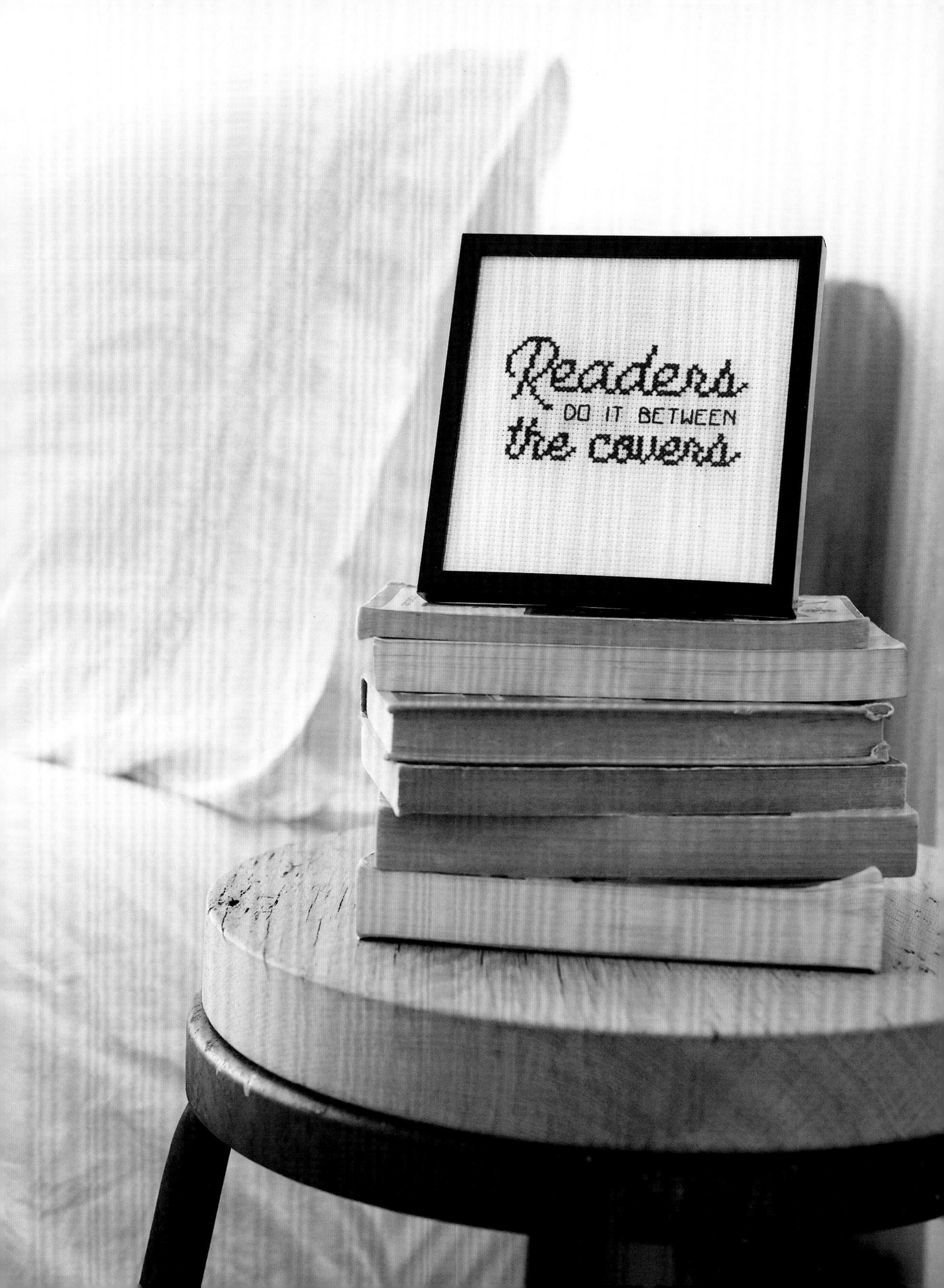
Readers
DO IT BETWEEN
the covers

| xxxxxxx | DMC 915 | Dark Plum | 2 strands | 5.77 yards |
| xxxxxxx | DMC 796 | Dark Royal Blue | 2 strands | 0.22 yards |

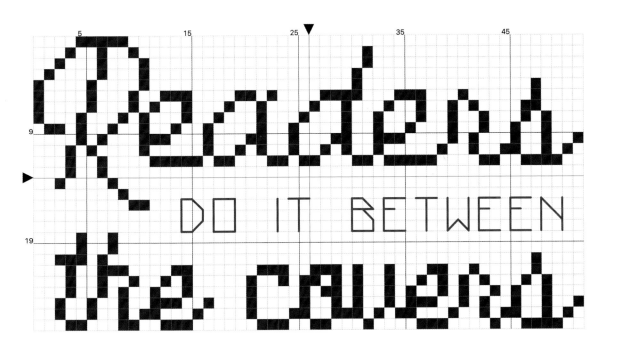

Readers
DO IT BETWEEN
the covers.

We've always thought that "bookworm" wasn't an exciting enough term to describe **something as rad as being a diehard book person**, but it seems like the term is here to stay. If you can't beat 'em, you might as well join 'em . . . with a pair of awesome knuckle tats. Put your best fist forward with an ink-inspired design.

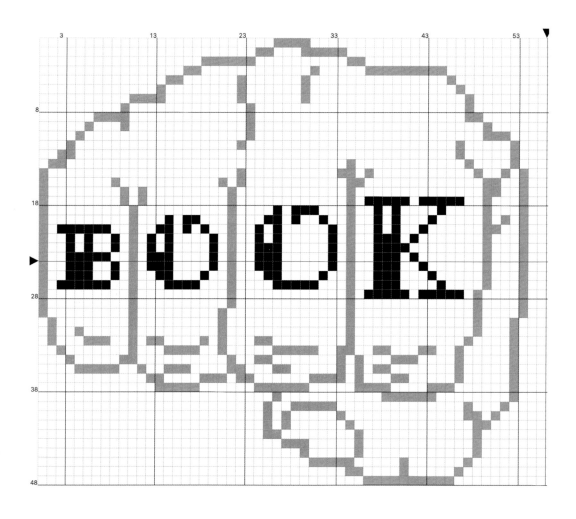

| xxxxxxx | DMC 741 | Medium Tangerine | 2 strands | 14.12 yards |
| **xxxxxxx** | DMC E310 | Metallic Black | 2 strands | 5.88 yards |

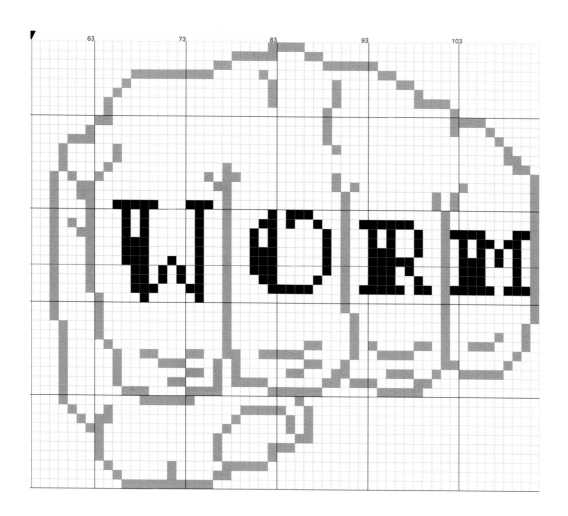

Oh, this one has so many applications! Whether the only thing you've lifted in recent memory is a hardcover, or you like to pick up heavy weights and put them down again (while listening to audiobooks, obviously), **you've got literary muscles to flex.** And who among us hasn't had a conversation that made us want to reply, "Ugh, don't you even read?" You get it.

xxxxxxx   DMC E310   Metallic Black   2 strands   24.92 yards

Books are inherently political, and they always have been. Literature shapes how we see the world, and the stories that are told (or not told) are both a cause and an effect of the society we live in. Books can teach us how to be more inclusive, how to make the world bigger and safer for more people, and how to move toward true equality. They are an essential tool of resistance. **They light a flame within us and give us a common language.** This design is about celebrating the revolutionary power of reading.

xxxxxxx	DMC E310	Metallic Black	2 strands	21.46 yards
xxxxxxx	DMC E321	Metallic Red Ruby	2 strands	1.42 yards
xxxxxxx	DMC 168	Very Light Pewter	2 strands	0.71 yards

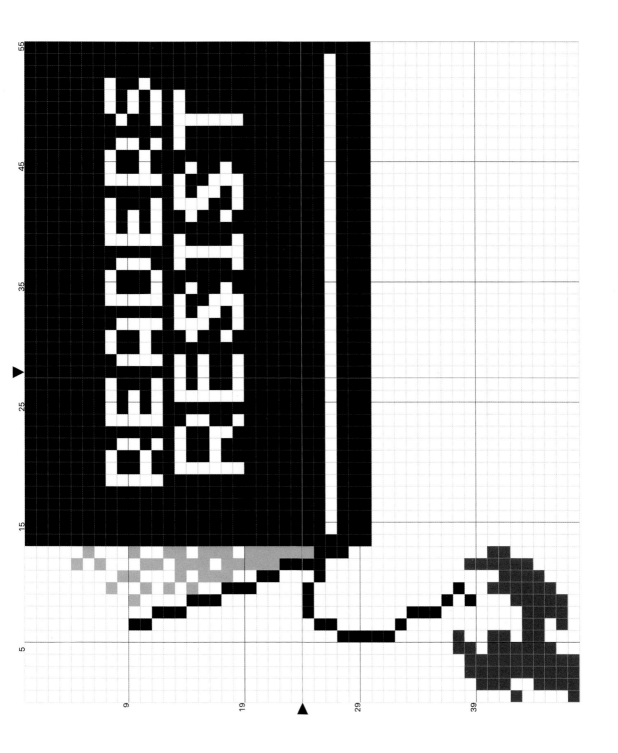

We've all been there: you go to put a book on the shelf, and there's no room left. But you don't want to get rid of any books, so what do you do? You start stacking. One stack begets another, until the stacks are no longer confined to the shelves, but take over coffee tables and bedside tables and desks and maybe, for the hardest of hardcore readers, the floor. Stacks on stacks? You betcha.

*Note: cut your piece of fabric to about 2.5 times the width of the bookmark and with an extra 2 inches (5 cm) on the ends that will be frayed.

XXXXXXX	DMC 158	Medium Cornflower Blue	2 strands	10.19 yards
XXXXXXX	DMC 817	Very Dark Coral Red	2 strands	6.23 yards
XXXXXXX	DMC 611	Drab Brown	2 strands	3.19 yards
XXXXXXX	DMC 435	Very Light Brown	2 strands	3.68 yards
XXXXXXX	DMC E3849	Metallic Aquamarine Blue	2 strands	3.42 yards
XXXXXXX	DMC E966	Metallic Lime	2 strands	1.51 yards

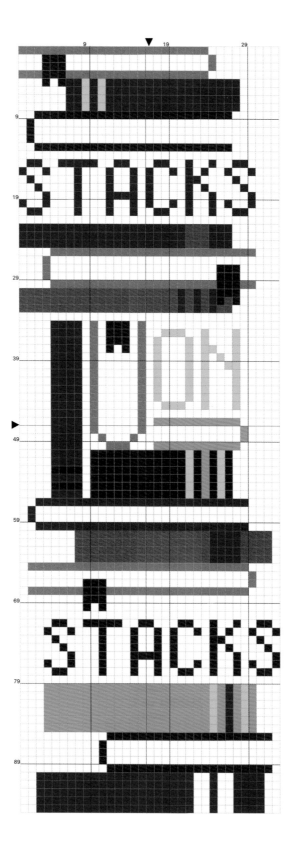

Okay, maybe you're not ready to commit to a big "I ♥ Books" tattoo (or, who knows, maybe you already have one!). Either way, let the edgier side of your bookish identity out for a joyride with this classic-ink-inspired design. Hang it on your office wall or display it proudly on your desk to **tell the world your heart belongs to books.**

xxxxxxx	DMC 310	Black	2 strands	10.07 yards
xxxxxxx	DMC 817	Very Dark Coral Red	2 strands	10.05 yards
xxxxxxx	DMC 815	Medium Garnet	2 strands	1.00 yard
xxxxxxx	DMC 3731	Very Dark Dusty Rose	2 strands	0.18 yards
xxxxxxx	DMC 987	Dark Forest Green	2 strands	1.04 yards
xxxxxxx	DMC 890	Ultra Dark Pistachio Green	2 strands	0.55 yards
xxxxxxx	DMC 772	Very Light Yellow Green	2 strands	0.16 yards
xxxxxxx	DMC 791	Very Dark Cornflower Blue	2 strands	0.39 yards
xxxxxxx	DMC 799	Medium Delft Blue	2 strands	0.18 yards
xxxxxxx	DMC 959	Medium Sea Green	2 strands	0.26 yards
xxxxxxx	DMC 598	Light Turquoise	2 strands	0.18 yards
xxxxxxx	DMC 972	Deep Canary	2 strands	0.89 yards

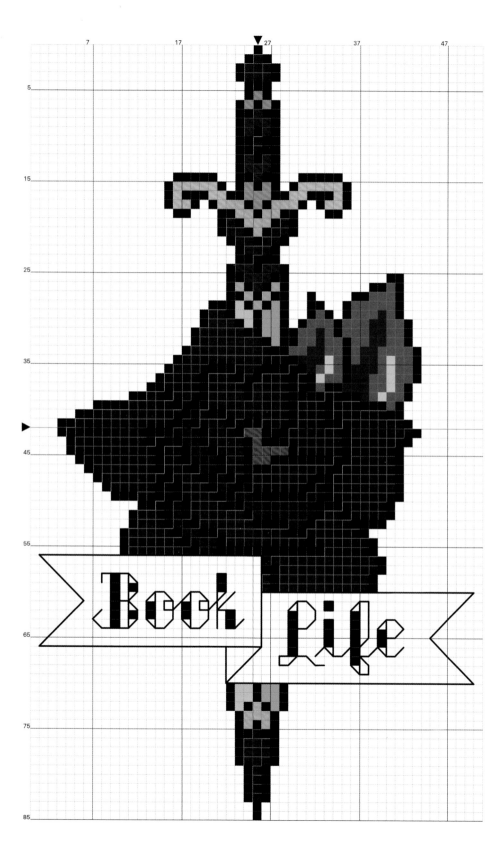

This one goes out to all the people who ask silly questions like, "So what do you do for fun *besides* reading?" Maybe you have a bunch of answers to that question, and if you do, that's rad.

But if reading is your main squeeze, you'll get no shade from us.

Think happy thoughts about your favorite book and channel them into this tribute to your favorite, most enjoyable way to spend time.

THERE IS NO
ENJOYMENT
LIKE READING
-JANE AUSTEN

EMMA
LITTLE WOMEN
MOBY DICK

xxxxxxx	DMC 991	Dark Aquamarine	2 strands	9.99 yards
xxxxxxx	DMC 992	Medium Aquamarine	2 strands	9.03 yards
xxxxxxx	DMC 3716	Very Light Dusty Rose	2 strands	2.62 yards
xxxxxxx	DMC 3731	Very Dark Dusty Rose	2 strands	5.19 yards
xxxxxxx	DMC 727	Very Light Topaz	2 strands	1.32 yards
xxxxxxx	DMC 728	Golden Yellow	2 strands	7.08 yards
xxxxxxx	DMC 3753	Ultra Very Light Antique Blue	2 strands	3.23 yards
xxxxxxx	DMC 157	Very Light Cornflower Blue	2 strands	2.24 yards
xxxxxxx	DMC E415	Metallic Pewter	2 strands	2.24 yards
xxxxxxx	DMC 310	Black	2 strands	0.38 yards

THERE IS NO ENJOYMENT LIKE READING

-JANE AUSTEN

EMMA

LITTLE WOMEN

MOBY DICK

The first rule of being a book lover is:

don't leave home without something to read.

Waiting in line or for an appointment can be annoying, or it can be an opportunity to squeeze in a few more pages. And if you're headed over to a party for the night? Well. You know the **real** meaning of **BYOB**, so go ahead and bring some of that, too.

xxxxxxx	DMC 986	Very Dark Forest Green	2 strands	18.45 yards
xxxxxxx	DMC 815	Medium Garnet	2 strands	17.39 yards
xxxxxxx	DMC 3750	Very Dark Antique Blue	2 strands	15.18 yards
xxxxxxx	DMC E310	Metallic Black	2 strands	4.82 yards
xxxxxxx	DMC 725	Topaz	2 strands	3.83 yards
xxxxxxx	DMC 993	Light Aquamarine	2 strands	1.10 yards

Like the curse word that features prominently in this design, this phrase has myriad uses. Maybe you've wanted to shout it at the person asking questions they should know the answers to. Maybe you're the only reader in your group of friends, and it would just be so nice if someone else would talk books with you sometime. Maybe, like us, you wish you could turn it into a flashing sign and display it at busy intersections. **Or maybe you simply appreciate a well-deployed swear.** You don't have to tell us your reason. Now, go make a fucking craft.

*Note: cut your piece of fabric to about 2.5 times the width of the bookmark and with an extra 2 inches (5 cm) on the ends that will be frayed.

xxxxxxx	DMC 986	Very Dark Forest Green	2 strands	4.11 yards
xxxxxxx	DMC 728	Golden Yellow	2 strands	3.58 yards

Read a fucking book

Sometimes
it's best to just
get right
to the point.

Books!

They're great.

*Note: cut your piece of fabric to about 2.5 times the width of the bookmark and with an extra 2 inches (5 cm) on the ends that will be frayed.

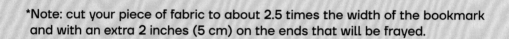 DMC E815   Metallic Dark Red Ruby   2 strands   8.86 yards

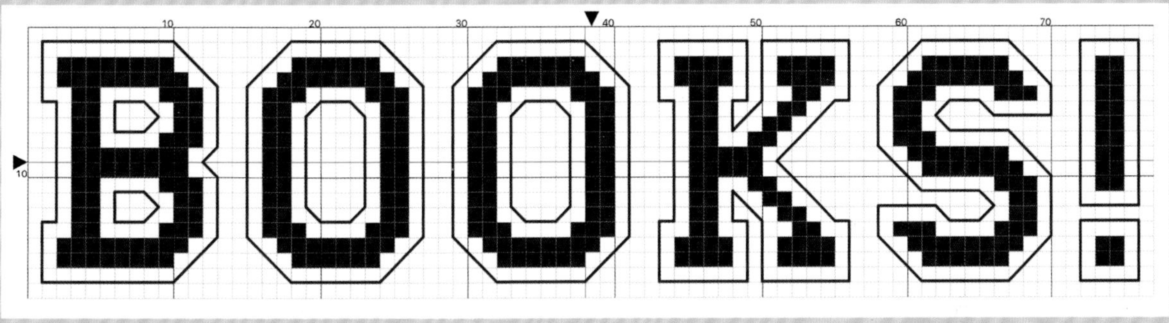
10
20
30
40
50
60
70
10

Book Riot has always believed that all the fun stuff around books and reading should be just as diverse as books and readers are. **All readers deserve to see their stories and experiences reflected back to them on the page, and the great big beautiful world is something to be celebrated.** Let your Pride shine with this whimsical stitching project.

*Note: cut your piece of fabric to about 2.5 times the width of the bookmark and with an extra 2 inches (5 cm) on the ends that will be frayed.

xxxxxxx	DMC 321	Red	2 strands	2.20 yards
xxxxxxx	DMC 970	Light Pumpkin	2 strands	2.20 yards
xxxxxxx	DMC 973	Bright Canary	2 strands	2.20 yards
xxxxxxx	DMC 505	Jade Green	2 strands	2.20 yards
xxxxxxx	DMC 825	Dark Blue	2 strands	2.20 yards
xxxxxxx	DMC 550	Very Dark Violet	2 strands	2.20 yards

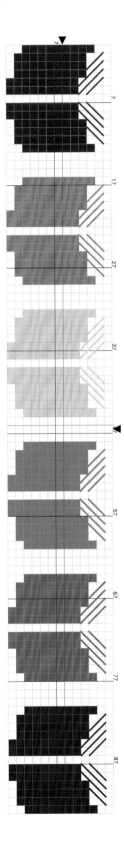

Close your eyes. Take a deep breath.

Imagine the perfect place— paradise, if you will. It has a lot of books, right? #nailedit. This is one of the most-loved quotes about literary life, and for good reason. Obviously, any paradise worth its name would have a never-ending supply of reading material. Conjure up dreams of your ideal reading spot, pick your prettiest thread, and make it happen.

*Note: use 3 strands of white floss instead of 2 for the backstitched words on this pattern, so that they show up more strongly against the blue fabric.

xxxxxxx	DMC BLANC 2 strands	White 44.09 yards
xxxxxxx	DMC 606 2 strands	Bright Orange-Red 7.06 yards
xxxxxxx	DMC 352 2 strands	Coral Light 0.94 yards
xxxxxxx	DMC 991 2 strands	Dark Aquamarine 2.99 yards
xxxxxxx	DMC 992 2 strands	Medium Aquamarine 3.58 yards
xxxxxxx	DMC 959 2 strands	Medium Sea Green 2.20 yards
xxxxxxx	DMC 964 2 strands	Light Sea Green 0.79 yards

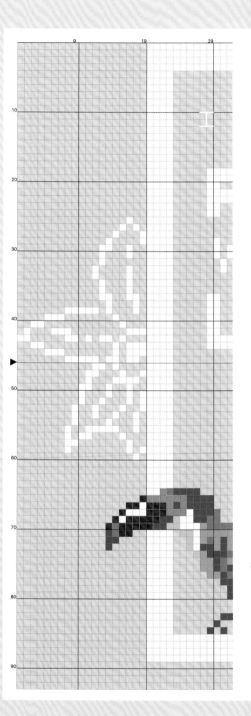

I HAVE ALWAYS IMAGINED
THAT
PARADISE
WILL BE A KIND OF
LIBRARY

-JORGE LUIS BORGES

Deck your halls with a festive design as you ring in the most wonderful time of the year!
(P.S.: It makes a great gift, too!)

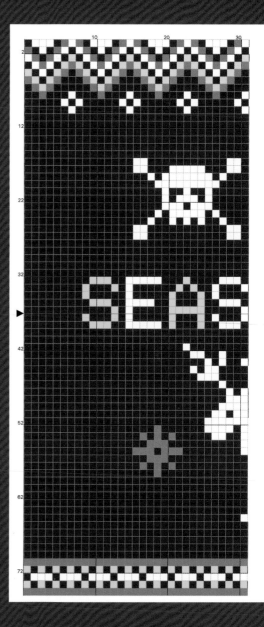

xxxxxxx DMC BLANC White
       2 strands   21.67 yards

xxxxxxx DMC 3815   Dark Celedon Green
       2 strands   12.51 yards

xxxxxxx DMC 964   Light Sea Green
       2 strands   7.30 yards

The only thing better than a good pun is a good bookish pun. **You have major heart-eyes for books, and everybody knows it.** So, make this for your bestie, your sweetie, and all the beautiful nerds in your book club, and make one for yourself too. After all, bookish gifts are the best gifts.

*Note: You can opt to leave the areas that call for Glow-in-the-Dark thread unstitched, in this case, as the fabric is white.

xxxxxxx	DMC E321	Metallic Red	2 strands	40.04 yards
	DMC E940	Glow-in-the-Dark	2 strands	1.53 yards
xxxxxxx	DMC 310	Black	2 strands	5.12 yards
xxxxxxx	DMC 725	Topaz	2 strands	1.46 yards
xxxxxxx	DMC 727	Very Light Topaz	2 strands	4.66 yards
xxxxxxx	DMC 209	Dark Lavender	2 strands	1.46 yards
xxxxxxx	DMC 211	Light Lavender	2 strands	4.66 yards

C. S. Lewis said,

"You can never get a cup of tea large enough or a book long enough to suit me."

If you second that emotion, this one's for you. Pour yourself a nice cuppa, settle into a comfy chair, and think cozy bookish thoughts while you stitch this soon-to-be classic.

xxxxxxx	DMC 3750	Very Dark Antique Blue	2 strands	15.08 yards
xxxxxxx	DMC 349	Dark Coral	2 strands	11.29 yards
xxxxxxx	DMC 563	Light Jade	2 strands	8.50 yards
xxxxxxx	DMC 799	Medium Delft Blue	2 strands	2.79 yards
xxxxxxx	DMC 3765	Dark Raspberry	2 strands	0.22 yards
	DMC BLANC	White	2 strands	0.59 yards

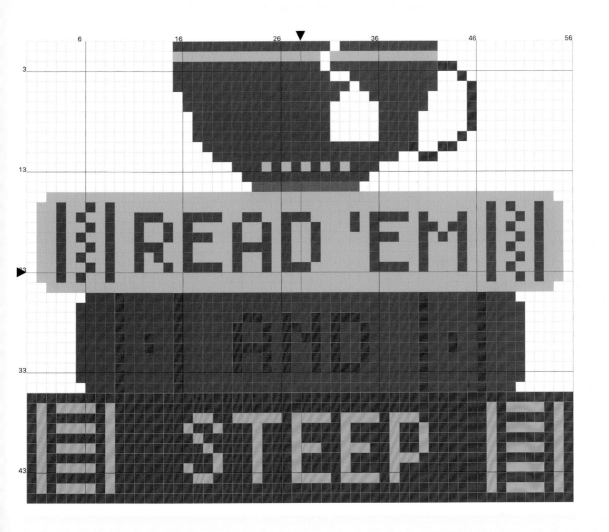

T. S. Eliot wrote about measuring life in coffee spoons, and honestly, that sounds like a pretty solid option. Maybe not better than measuring it in books or pages, but high on the list. Or, you know, do both! **Because books and coffee are BFFs.**

XXXXXXX	DMC 3031	Very Dark Mocha Brown	2 strands	17.56 yards
XXXXXXX	DMC 167	Very Dark Yellow Beige	2 strands	3.72 yards

Look, we know your TBR list is probably miles long, and you don't really *need* that book you're eyeing. But we're in no position to judge. Go ahead and treat yourself. Er. Your shelf. You know what? Just go for it.

xxxxxxxxxx

XXXXXXXX	DMC E815	Metallic Dark Red Ruby	2 strands	14.81 yards
XXXXXXXX	DMC 826	Medium Blue	2 strands	14.36 yards
XXXXXXXX	DMC 796	Dark Royal Blue	2 strands	9.30 yards
XXXXXXXX	DMC 208	Very Dark Lavender	2 strands	4.20 yards
XXXXXXXX	DMC 964	Light Sea Green	2 strands	3.68 yards
XXXXXXXX	DMC 992	Medium Aquamarine	2 strands	2.04 yards

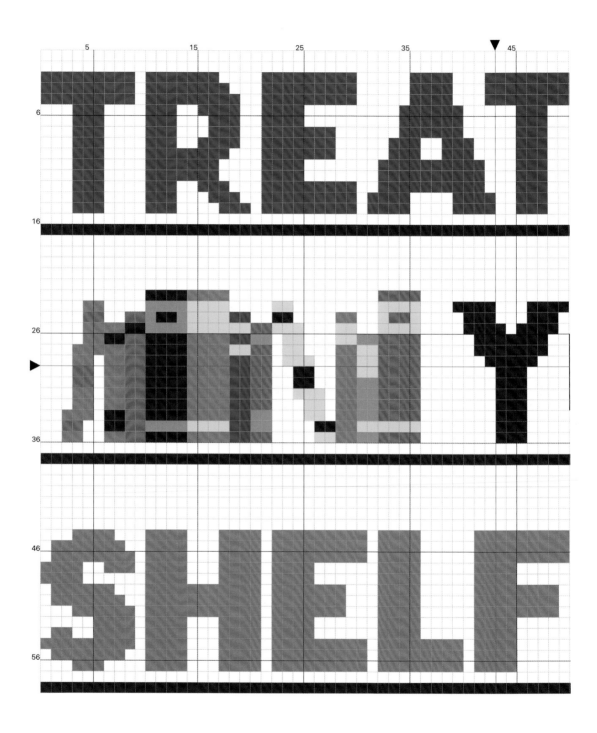

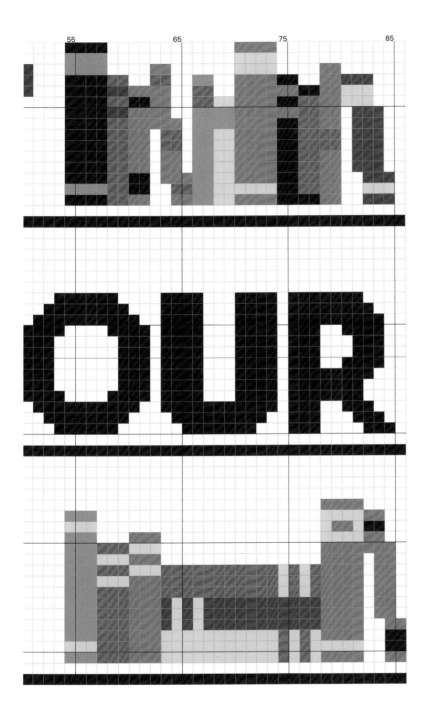

Since we're already on the record as thinking that "bookworm" isn't an exciting enough term for diehard readers, let's just go ahead and propose that it be replaced with **bookasaurus** instead. What's cooler than a dinosaur? Nothing.

xxxxxxxxxx

xxxxxxx	DMC 3760	Medium Wedgewood	2 strands	50.72 yards
xxxxxxx	DMC 3842	Dark Wedgwood	2 strands	4.05 yards
xxxxxxx	DMC 3846	Bright Light Turquoise	2 strands	8.55 yards
xxxxxxx	DMC 156	Medium Light Blue Violet	2 strands	6.53 yards
xxxxxxx	DMC 350	Medium Coral	2 strands	8.99 yards
xxxxxxx	DMC 760	Salmon	2 strands	8.48 yards
	DMC BLANC	White	2 strands	0.73 yards

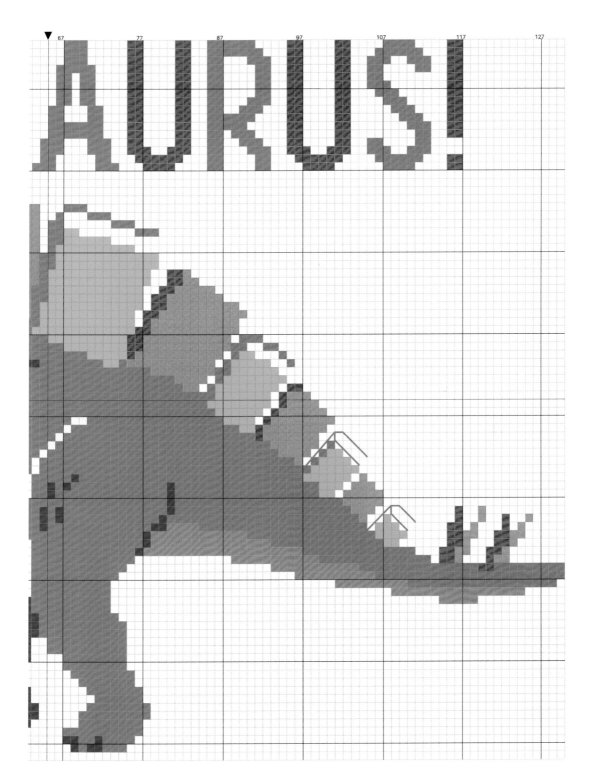

It is a truth universally acknowledged that life includes a certain amount of, well, bullshit. Homework. Taxes. Dishes. Laundry. That coworker who doesn't do their fair share of group projects. The neighbors who don't pick up after their dog. Ugh! It's the desire of every reader's heart to spend more time with books and less time with the bullshit, so we figured, why not put it in a cross-stitch?

xxxxxxx	DMC 349	Dark Coral	2 strands	5.76 yards
xxxxxxx	DMC 826	Medium Blue	2 strands	2.79 yards
xxxxxxx	DMC 728	Golden Yellow	2 strands	1.10 yards
xxxxxxx	DMC E310	Metallic Black	2 strands	0.61 yards

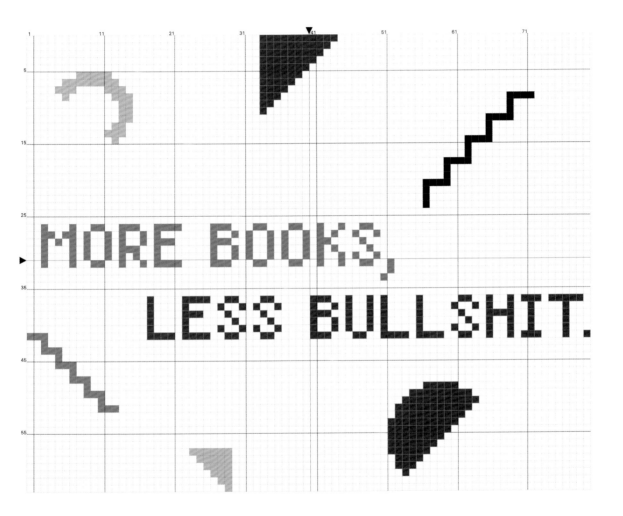

MORE BOOKS,
LESS BULLSHIT.

What do we really need to say about this one?

It DOES feel good to be a reader.

If you didn't think so, you wouldn't be here, making a cross-stitch about how good it feels, right? We tip our hats to *Office Space* for inspiring this one. Never seen it? No matter. You're an OG book nerd, and that's all you need to get by.

| xxxxxxx | DMC 959 | Medium Sea Green | 2 strands | 7.83 yards |
| xxxxxxx | DMC 939 | Very Dark Navy Blue | 2 strands | 2.42 yards |

DAMN, IT FEELS GOOD TO BE A READER.

You like old books,
and you cannot lie.
Celebrate the classics
with irreverent style.

DMC E940   Glow-in-the-Dark   2 strands   21.59 yards

If bookworms had a biker gang,

this would be the logo.

The members would stock their sidecars with beloved titles and zip around town stocking little free libraries and filling community shelves in their favorite coffee shops. Sure, snuggling up in a cozy chair with a plush blanket and a big cup of tea is a great way to be a reader, but it's not the only way. And who says you can only be one thing, anyway? Express the hard-core side of your reading personality with this design.

xxxxxxx	DMC BLANC	White	2 strands	22.42 yards
xxxxxxx	DMC 349	Dark Coral	2 strands	5.03 yards

READ
OR
DIE

Be honest. If you were driving down the highway and saw a sign flashing BOOKS BOOKS BOOKS in neon lights, you'd pull over. A full bookshelf calls out to you with a siren song, beckoning you into the bookstore, where you hand over your credit card and your last shreds of willpower. Let your literary love shine bright.

*Note: To get a more neon-like effect, you can use metallic/fluorescent threads such as DMC Light Effects.

XXXXXXXX	DMC BLANC	White	2 strands	22.03 yards
XXXXXXXX	DMC 603	Medium Pink Mauve	2 strands	20.28 yards

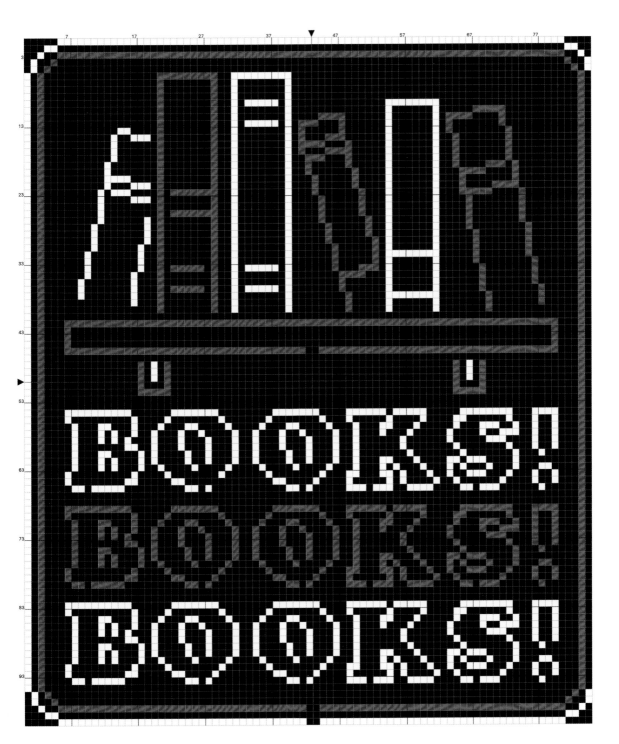

Resources & Acknowledgments